Franchise Accounting

Steven M. Bragg

 **Accounting**Tools®

Published by AccountingTools, Inc., Centennial, Colorado.

No part of this publication may be reproduced, stored in a retrieval system, or transmitted in any form or by any means, except as permitted under Section 107 or 108 of the 1976 United States Copyright Act, without the prior written permission of the Publisher. Requests to the Publisher for permission should be addressed to Steven M. Bragg, 6727 E. Fremont Place, Centennial, CO 80112.

Limit of Liability/Disclaimer of Warranty: While the publisher and author have used their best efforts in preparing this book, they make no representations or warranties with respect to the accuracy or completeness of the contents of this book and specifically disclaim any implied warranties of merchantability or fitness for a particular purpose. No warranty may be created or extended by written sales materials. The advice and strategies contained herein may not be suitable for your situation. You should consult with a professional where appropriate. Neither the publisher nor author shall be liable for any loss of profit or any other commercial damages, including but not limited to special, incidental, consequential, or other damages.

ISBN 978-1-64221-152-8

For more information about AccountingTools® products, visit our Web site at www.accountingtools.com.

Table of Contents

About the Author

Steven Bragg, CPA, has been the chief financial officer or controller of four companies, as well as a consulting manager at Ernst & Young. He received a master's degree in finance from Bentley College, an MBA from Babson College, and a Bachelor's degree in Economics from the University of Maine. He has been a two-time president of the Colorado Mountain Club, and is an avid alpine skier, mountain biker, and certified master diver. Mr. Bragg resides in Centennial, Colorado. He has written more than 300 books and courses, including *New Controller Guidebook, GAAP Guidebook,* and *Payroll Management.* He has also written the science fiction novel *Under an Autumn Sun,* first book in *The Auditors* trilogy.

Steven maintains the accountingtools.com web site, which contains continuing professional education courses, the Accounting Best Practices podcast, and thousands of articles on accounting subjects.

Franchise Accounting

Introduction

A franchise is a privilege granted to a third party to market a good or service, usually under a trademarked name. The key parties in a franchising arrangement are the franchisor and the franchisee. The franchisor is the party that grants business rights related to a franchise to the franchisee, which is the party that commits to operate the franchised entity. The franchisee pays a fee to the franchisor, which is typically based on a percentage of the sales generated by the franchisee. This arrangement can be somewhat more accurately called business format franchising, where the franchisor has perfected a replicable business model that it commits to teach to its franchisees, along with a solid system of controls.

In this manual, we explore those accounting issues that are specific to the accounting for franchisors and franchisees, including such matters as program development costs, cooperative advertising funds, and franchise renewal fees. Some of the information in this manual is derived from Section 952 of the Accounting Standards Codification, *Franchisors*.

The Franchising Process

A prospective franchisor begins by developing a business model that it believes can be readily replicated, with each outlet being able to earn a profit as long as it follows the established business model. To do so, the franchisor may spend several years developing its business model and training program, while also securing a trademark to protect its name. Once this phase is complete, the franchisor initiates a selling campaign to market its franchise program to prospective franchisees. The general types of arrangements being sold are:

- *Single unit*. In this arrangement, the franchisee invests his own capital and becomes the hands-on manager of a franchise that covers a specific geographic region. The agreement is for a specific period of time, such as ten years, after which it expires. If the franchisee wants to renew at the end of the current contract, it will need to pay a renewal fee, as well as bring its facilities up to the franchisor's current standards.
- *Multi-unit*. In an *area development franchising* arrangement, the franchisee obtains the right to develop a certain number of units within a defined territory, such as a county or state. This entity then enters into a separate arrangement with the franchisor for each unit constructed within that territory. A variation on this concept is the *master franchising agreement*, where the franchisor grants another party (the master franchisee) the right to sub-franchise to an additional level of franchisees. A master franchising agreement tends to cover a larger region than is typically found for an area development

1

franchise. Since the capital of sub-franchisees can be accessed to build out additional units, a master franchising agreement tends to result in a faster rollout of a franchising concept.

Once a franchisee signs on to the program, it is required to:

- Use the franchisor's logo
- Exclusively sell the franchisor's products and services
- Adhere to the business processes taught by the franchisor

To start up a franchise, the franchisor may provide the franchisee with a turnkey solution, where the franchisor finds a location, builds it out, stocks it with inventory, and hands over the facility to the franchisee. In return for this substantial amount of work, the franchisee pays the franchisor a significant fee that includes the cost of any inventory provided. A variation on this concept is for the franchisor to directly operate a unit for a period of time, before handing it over to a franchisee. A different approach is for the franchisee to be involved in the development process, with the oversight and approval of the franchisor. Doing so increases the risk of failure for the franchisee, since the location of the unit is untested. A final startup possibility is for an independent business to enter into a franchisee relationship, where it agrees to operate under the logo of the franchisor. In this last arrangement, the franchisee already knows that the selected location can succeed, since it has already been in operation for some time, and can now benefit from the franchisor's local and national advertising campaigns.

Fees Associated with a Franchise Agreement

There are several fees associated with a franchise agreement. First, the franchisee will be required to pay an up-front fee, which is used to fund the franchisor's costs to set up the franchisee. These costs may include:

- Property location services
- Property lease negotiations
- Site development
- Training provided to the franchisee
- Initial marketing promotions

If the franchisee is entering into an area development franchising agreement, the franchisor typically requires that the related area development fee be paid up front, though this may be delayed until each unit within the area is actually opened for business. When the franchisee is instead agreeing to a master franchising agreement, the master franchisee is usually required to pay the related master franchising fee up front, as well as a franchise fee for each unit as it is opened.

In addition, there is a recurring franchise fee that is based on the gross revenues generated by the franchisee. This fee is used to pay for the various services provided by the franchisor to the franchisee on an ongoing basis. Examples of these services are providing operating assistance, accounting services, and engaging in product development activities. The franchisor usually earns a profit from both types of fees.

Franchisor Accounting Issues

The franchisor may confront a number of accounting issues that are unique to the franchising process, which are addressed in this section.

Franchise Program Development Costs

A franchisor will likely incur significant up-front costs to develop its franchise, so that it can earn revenues from its franchise operations over time. These costs are generally considered to be research and development costs, which are to be charged to expense as incurred. An alternative viewpoint is that these costs are really intangible assets that should be capitalized. However, internally-developed intangible assets must be charged to expense as incurred, so there is still no allowable capitalization of these expenditures.

See the later Contract-Related Costs section for a discussion of how to account for the selling activities associated with the recruiting of franchisees, some of which can be capitalized.

Security Deposits

If a franchisor is routinely selling goods to its franchisees, it may end up extending a substantial amount of trade credit to the franchisees. To keep from incurring significant bad debts from these credit sales, the franchisor may require that franchisees pay it a security deposit. If so, the franchisor holds the related funds in a liability account. Since these deposits may not be paid back for years (if ever), the account should be classified on the franchisor's balance sheet as long-term.

Construction Payments

In many franchising situations, the franchisor constructs a facility on behalf of the franchisee, with the franchisee paying the franchisor advances as the work progresses. In addition, the franchisor may charge the franchisee a fee to manage the construction process. The franchisor records these payments in a development fund liability account, against which construction billings are then charged.

EXAMPLE

Bigelow Burgers enters into a franchise agreement with Lucky Star Ventures to open a franchise in Albuquerque. Bigelow will be in charge of the construction and outfitting of the facility, which will require four months to complete. Lucky Star sends Bigelow a $100,000 advance, which Bigelow records as follows:

	Debit	Credit
Cash [asset]	100,000	
Development fund [liability]		100,000

A contractor then sends Bigelow an initial billing for $56,000, which Bigelow pays and charges against the fund with the following entry:

	Debit	Credit
Development fund [liability]	56,000	
Cash [asset]		56,000

Alternatively, the construction billings can be initially compiled by the franchisor into a construction-in-progress asset account, which is then netted against the development fund when construction is complete.

Continuing Franchise Fees

Continuing franchise fees are those fees charged by a franchisor to a franchisee in exchange for the continuing rights granted to the franchisee under the terms of a franchise agreement. When the franchisor incurs costs related to these continuing fees, it should charge them to expense as incurred. These costs are likely to include nearly all operating costs of the business, such as general, selling, and administrative expenses.

Cooperative Advertising Fund

A franchisor frequently requires its franchisees to contribute to a cooperative advertising fund, which it then uses to engage in advertising activities on behalf of the franchisees. The franchisor also contributes to this fund on behalf of its company-owned units. The amount contributed is usually a percentage of the gross sales of each unit.

Advertising funds are usually collected first and then expended by the franchisor; this means that the funds collected are initially a liability of the franchisor. The reverse situation is also possible, where the franchisor initially expends its own funds for advertising on behalf of franchisees, after which funds received from them are used to pay down their liability to the franchisor. In the latter case, the franchisor might charge interest to the franchisees. The franchisor may also be able to charge overhead and administrative costs to the fund. The franchisor is required by the underlying franchise agreement to periodically report back to the franchisees about how their advertising funds were used.

EXAMPLE

The franchise agreement for Bigelow Burgers requires that all franchisees pay 4% of their gross revenues into a cooperative advertising fund that is managed by Bigelow. In March, a franchisee pays $14,000 into the fund, for which Bigelow's entry is:

	Debit	Credit
Cash [asset]	14,000	
Franchise advertising fund [liability]		14,000

During the month, Bigelow pays an advertising agency a $10,000 progress payment against its development of a new ad campaign. The entry is:

	Debit	Credit
Franchise advertising fund [liability]	10,000	
Cash [asset]		10,000

Under the terms of the franchise agreement, Bigelow is allowed to charge the fund $8,000 each month as an administrative charge for the staff time required to manage advertising activities. The entry is:

	Debit	Credit
Franchise advertising fund [liability]	8,000	
Compensation expense [expense]		8,000

Costs of Franchisor-Owned Outlets

When a franchisor owns some of its outlets while operating through franchisees in other locations, it should distinguish between the costs related to the franchised outlets and the other incurred costs.

Repurchase or Reacquisition of a Franchise by the Franchisor

A franchisor may have the right to repurchase a franchise from a franchisee. If it chooses to do so, it typically acquires the franchisee as a going concern, paying fair market value for the franchisee entity, possibly including a price increase that represents the goodwill associated with a successful franchise operation. When this happens, the accounting depends on the intent of the franchisor. The options are:

- *Closure.* When the purchased franchise will not be kept in operation, the franchisor apportions the purchase price among the assets and liabilities acquired, based on their relative fair market values. If the aggregate amount of the asset and liability fair values is less than the price paid by the franchisor, the difference is charged to expense. Any acquisition costs are charged to expense.

- *Ongoing*. When the franchisor intends to continue operating the acquired franchisee units, the transaction is considered a business combination. Under this scenario, the total cost of the acquisition is the amount of consideration paid, plus any acquisition costs and unamortized initial franchise fees. This total acquisition cost is then allocated to all identifiable assets and liabilities based on their fair values. If the total cost exceeds the fair market value of the reacquired assets and liabilities, the difference is allocated to the goodwill intangible asset. See the author's *Business Combinations and Consolidations* course for more information.

- *Refranchise*. When the franchisor intends to sell an acquired franchise as soon as it can find a replacement franchisee, the reacquired assets are classified as held for sale. This designation allows the franchisor to hold the assets without depreciating them, though only if the following criteria are met:
  - Management commits to a plan to sell the assets.
  - The assets are available for sale immediately in their present condition.
  - There is an active program to sell the assets.
  - It is unlikely that the plan to sell the assets will be changed or withdrawn.
  - Sale of the assets is likely to occur, and should be completed within one year.
  - The assets are being marketed at a price that is considered reasonable in comparison to their current fair value.

If assets are classified as held for sale, measure them at the lower of their carrying amount or their fair value minus any cost to sell. If it is necessary to write down the carrying amount of an asset to its fair value minus any cost to sell, then recognize a loss in the amount of the write down.

Sale of a Franchisor-Owned Unit

A franchisor may initially operate a unit, and then sells it to a franchisee. When the unit is already operating in an unusually profitable manner, this represents a goodwill factor that increases the amount charged to the eventual purchaser of the franchise. When this is the case, the franchisor should split the price paid by the new franchisee into the initial franchise fee and the goodwill portion of the transaction. Any booked costs associated with the unit are then offset against the goodwill portion of the transaction to arrive at a net gain.

EXAMPLE

Bigelow Burgers starts up a company-owned concept store in Kalamazoo, and rapidly builds it into one of its most profitable stores anywhere in the country. It then sells the store to a franchisee. The total price charged is $1,500,000, of which $50,000 is the initial franchise fee. Bigelow has accumulated $600,000 of costs related to the construction and outfitting of the store. Bigelow's accountant subtracts the $50,000 franchise fee from the $1,500,000 sale price to arrive at the $1,450,000 portion of the sale related to goodwill, and then subtracts out the $600,000 of booked costs to derive an $850,000 gain on sale of the company-owned unit.

Franchisee Accounting Issues

The franchisee may confront several accounting issues that are unique to the franchising process, which are addressed in this section.

Initial Franchise Fees and Area Development Fees

When a franchisee pays a franchise fee to a franchisor, this payment can be considered an intangible asset. It is permissible for the franchisee to recognize this cost as an asset, since it is an asset acquired from a third party. The franchisee should amortize this asset over its estimated useful life, which is presumed to be the term of the franchise agreement.

EXAMPLE

Furtive Development enters into a franchise arrangement with Bigelow Burgers, paying an upfront fee of $50,000. Furtive records the payment as follows:

	Debit	Credit
Franchise fee [asset]	50,000	
Cash [asset]		50,000

The franchise agreement has a term of 10 years, so Furtive amortizes the fee over 10 years on a straight-line basis. The first-year entry to record this amortization is:

	Debit	Credit
Amortization expense [expense]	5,000	
Accumulated amortization [contra asset]		5,000

This intangible asset should be tested for impairment at least annually. If the carrying amount of the asset exceeds its fair value, write the remaining balance down to its fair value. In the assessment of impairment, review all events and circumstances that could affect the determination of fair value, such as:

- Increases in costs that could negatively impact earnings and cash flows
- Declines in actual or planned revenue
- Regulatory, legal, contractual and other factors that limit fair value
- Litigation
- Management changes or the loss of key personnel
- Decline in the business environment or general economic conditions

EXAMPLE

After three years, Furtive Development has still not constructed the burger franchise location that it is entitled to construct under its franchise agreement with Bigelow Burgers, due to the intractability of the local zoning board in granting a zoning waiver to Furtive. Management concludes that there is no reasonable probability of ever being able to do so, resulting in the write-off of the remaining $35,000 of the franchise fee asset. The related journal entry is:

	Debit	Credit
Impairment loss [expense]	35,000	
Accumulated impairment losses [contra asset]		35,000

Furtive's accountant then removes the franchise fee asset from the firm's accounting records with the following entry:

	Debit	Credit
Accumulated impairment losses [contra asset]	35,000	
Accumulated amortization [contra asset]	15,000	
Franchise fee [asset]		50,000

Franchise Renewal Fees

A franchisee may be required to pay a renewal fee to extend the term of the original franchise agreement. The accounting for this fee is the same as was used for the initial franchise fee.

Capital Expenditures

A franchisee is likely to make a large number of purchases for items that can be classified as fixed assets. These assets should all be depreciated over their useful lives, less any estimated salvage value. The types of asset categories that may be used to classify these expenditures are noted in the following table.

Sample Franchisee Fixed Asset Classifications

Type of Expenditure	Fixed Asset Classification
Alterations to a leased location	Leasehold improvements
Furniture purchases, including delivery and installation costs	Furniture and fixtures
Equipment purchases, including delivery and installation costs	Equipment
Automobiles and vans, including alterations, licenses, and signage	Vehicles
Signs, including installation costs	Signage

Ongoing Expenditures

Other than payments for fixed assets, the ongoing expenditures of a franchisee are primarily charged to expense as incurred. The expense classifications used will be highly dependent on the type of franchise, but can be expected to include the following accounts:

- Compensation expense
- Employee benefits
- Franchisor royalty fees
- Insurance expense
- Legal and accounting expense
- Payroll taxes
- Promotions and advertising expense
- Rent expense
- Supplies expense
- Telephone expense
- Training expense
- Utilities expense

Payment of Transfer Fee

A franchisee may sell out to a replacement franchisee, which typically calls for the payment of a transfer fee to the franchisor. The outgoing franchisee can account for this fee as a cost of selling the business, which is therefore deducted from the gross proceeds of the sale.

Contract-Related Costs

A franchisor may incur several types of costs in order to complete a contract arrangement. In this section, we separately address the accounting for the costs incurred to initially obtain a contract, and how these costs are to be charged to expense.

Costs to Obtain a Contract

A franchisor may incur certain costs to obtain a contract. If so, it is allowable to record these costs as an asset and amortize them over the life of the contract. The following conditions apply:

- The costs must be incremental; that is, they would not have been incurred if the franchisor had not obtained the contract.
- If the amortization period will be one year or some lesser period, it is allowable to simply charge these costs to expense as incurred.
- There is an expectation that the costs will be recovered.

An example of a contract-related cost that could be recorded as an asset and amortized is the sales commission associated with selling a franchise, though as a practical expedient it is usually charged to expense as incurred.

EXAMPLE

A hamburger franchising firm works with a large prospective franchisor to develop an area franchise covering Montana and Idaho. The franchisor incurs the following costs as part of the contract development process:

Staff time to prepare preliminary contract	$18,000
Printing fees	2,500
Travel costs	5,000
Commissions paid to sales staff	15,000
	$40,500

The franchisor must charge the staff time, printing fees, and travel costs to expense as incurred, since it would have incurred these expenses even if the contractual arrangement had failed. Only the commissions paid to the sales staff can be considered a contract asset, since that cost should be recovered through its future billings for continuing franchise fees.

Amortization of Costs

When contract-related costs have been recognized as assets, they should be amortized on a systematic basis that reflects the timing of the transfer of related goods and services to the franchisee. If there is a change in the anticipated timing of the transfer of goods and services to the franchisee, update the amortization to reflect this change. This is considered a change in accounting estimate.

Impairment of Costs

The franchisor should recognize an impairment loss in the current period when the carrying amount of an asset associated with a contract is greater than the remaining payments to be received from the franchisee. The calculation is:

Remaining consideration to be received[1] – Costs not yet recognized as expenses

= Impairment amount (if result is a negative figure)

> **Note:** When calculating possible impairment, adjust the amount of the remaining consideration to be received for the effects of the franchisee's credit risk.

It is not allowable to reverse an impairment loss on contract assets that have already been recognized.

Franchisor Revenue Recognition

A franchisor can potentially accept a variety of payments that can be recognized as revenue, including the following:

- *Initial franchise fee*. Covers the provision of initial services to the franchisee, while also reimbursing the franchisor for the costs related to establishing the relationship. Initial services may include site selection, facility leasing activities, facility development, training costs, opening assistance, and initial advertising. It also provides some compensation for the franchisor's initial development costs.
- *Continuing franchise fees*. This is primarily comprised of a royalty fee that is calculated as a percentage of franchisee gross revenues. The franchisor may also charge its franchisees for special assistance in such areas as accounting, human resources, and training services.
- *Transfer fees to shift franchises to new franchisees*. The franchisor is entitled to charge a fee to an existing franchisee when the franchisee wants to sell its business to a new franchisee. It is payable by the selling franchisee to the franchisor prior to the ownership transfer.
- *Franchise renewal fees*. The franchisee is usually required to pay a franchise renewal fee in order to extend the term of the initial franchise agreement. The fee is intended to cover the franchisor's costs in overseeing upgrades to the franchisee's premises, as well as for retraining the staff.

---

[1] The remaining consideration to be received includes the residual amount expected to be received in the future and the amount already received but which has not yet been recognized as revenue.

The recognition rules for all of these types of revenue are governed by Topic 606 of the Accounting Standards Codification, *Revenue from Contracts with Customers*. Topic 606 establishes a series of actions that an entity takes to determine the amount and timing of revenue to be recognized. The main steps are:

1. Link the contract with a specific customer.
2. Note the performance obligations required by the contract.
3. Determine the price of the underlying transaction.
4. Match this price to the performance obligations through an allocation process.
5. Recognize revenue as the various obligations are fulfilled.

Step one, linking a contract to a specific customer, is not usually difficult for the franchisor, since there is a completed, signed contract with each individual franchisee. Step two, noting performance obligations, is also not difficult, since they are (or should be) stated in detail in the franchise agreement. Step three, determining the price of the transaction, is not difficult, since it is stated in the franchise agreement.

The problem arises in step four, where prices must be assigned to the franchisor's performance obligations. The basic rule is to allocate that price to a performance obligation that best reflects the amount of consideration to which the franchisor expects to be entitled when it satisfies each performance obligation. To determine this allocation, it is first necessary to estimate the standalone selling price of those distinct goods or services as of the inception date of the contract. If it is not possible to derive a standalone selling price, the franchisor must estimate it. This estimation should involve all relevant information that is reasonably available, such as:

- Competitive pressure on prices
- Costs incurred to manufacture or provide the item
- Item profit margins
- Pricing of other items in the same contract
- Standalone selling price of the item
- Supply and demand for the items in the market
- The franchisor's pricing strategy and practices
- The type of customer, distribution channel, or geographic region
- Third-party pricing

The following three approaches are acceptable ways in which to estimate a standalone selling price:

- *Adjusted market assessment.* This involves reviewing the market to estimate the price at which a customer in that market would be willing to pay for the goods and services in question. This can involve an examination of the prices of competitors for similar items and adjusting them to incorporate the franchisor's costs and margins.
- *Expected cost plus a margin.* This requires the franchisor to estimate the costs required to fulfill a performance obligation, and then add a margin to it to derive the estimated price.

- *Residual approach*. This involves subtracting all of the observable standalone selling prices from the total transaction price to arrive at the residual price remaining for allocation to any non-observable selling prices. This method can only be used if one of the following situations applies:
  - o The franchisor sells the good or service to other customers for a wide range of prices; or
  - o No price has yet been established for that item, and it has not yet been sold on a standalone basis.

The residual approach can be difficult to use when there are several goods or services with uncertain standalone selling prices. If so, it may be necessary to use a combination of methods to derive standalone selling prices, which should be used in the following order:

1. Estimate the aggregate amount of the standalone selling prices for all items having uncertain standalone selling prices, using the residual method.
2. Use another method to develop standalone selling prices for each item in this group, to allocate the aggregate amount of the standalone selling prices.

Once all standalone selling prices have been determined, allocate the transaction price amongst these distinct goods or services based on their relative standalone selling prices. Once the franchisor derives an approach for estimating a standalone selling price, it should consistently apply that method to the derivation of the standalone selling prices for other goods or services with similar characteristics.

This leaves us with step five, which is to recognize revenue as the various obligations are fulfilled. Revenue is to be recognized as goods or services are transferred to the franchisee. This transference is considered to occur when the franchisee gains control over the good or service. Indicators of this date include the following:

- When the franchisor has the right to receive payment.
- When the franchisee has legal title to the transferred asset.
- When physical possession of the asset has been transferred by the franchisor.
- When the franchisee has taken on the significant risks and rewards of ownership related to the asset transferred by the franchisor. For example, the franchisee can now sell, pledge, or exchange the asset.
- When the franchisee accepts the asset.
- When the franchisee can prevent other entities from using or obtaining benefits from the asset.

It is possible that a performance obligation will be transferred over time, rather than as of a specific point in time. If so, revenue recognition occurs when any one of the following criteria are met:

- *Immediate use*. The franchisee both receives and consumes the benefit provided by the franchisor as performance occurs. This situation arises if another entity would not need to re-perform work completed to date if the other entity were to take over the remaining performance obligation. Routine and recurring services typically fall into this classification.

- *Immediate enhancement.* The franchisor creates or enhances an asset controlled by the franchisee as performance occurs. This asset can be tangible or intangible.
- *No alternative use.* The franchisor's performance does not create an asset for which there is an alternative use to the franchisor (such as selling it to a different customer). In addition, the contract gives the franchisor an enforceable right to payment for the performance that has been completed to date. A lack of alternative use happens when a contract restricts the franchisor from directing the asset to another use, or when there are practical limitations on doing so, such as the incurrence of significant economic losses to direct the asset elsewhere. The determination of whether an asset has an alternative use is made at the inception of the contract, and cannot be subsequently altered unless both parties to the contract approve a modification that results in a substantive change in the performance obligation.

When a performance obligation is being completed over a period of time, the franchisor recognizes revenue through the application of a progress completion method. The goal of this method is to determine the progress of the franchisor in achieving complete satisfaction of its performance obligation. This method is to be consistently applied over time, and shall be re-measured at the end of each reporting period.

Both output methods and input methods are considered acceptable for determining progress completion. The method chosen should incorporate due consideration of the nature of the goods or services being provided to the franchisee. An output method recognizes revenue based on a comparison of the value to the franchisee of goods and services transferred to date to the remaining goods and services not yet transferred. There are numerous ways to measure output, including:

- Surveys of performance to date
- Milestones reached
- The passage of time
- The number of units delivered
- The number of units produced

Another output method that may be acceptable is the amount of consideration that the franchisor has the right to invoice, such as billable hours. This approach works when the franchisor has a right to invoice an amount that matches the amount of performance completed to date.

An input method derives the amount of revenue to be recognized based on the to-date effort required by the franchisor to satisfy a performance obligation relative to the total estimated amount of effort required. Examples of possible inputs are costs incurred and labor hours expended.

> **Tip:** If the effort expended to satisfy performance obligations occurs evenly through the performance period, consider recognizing revenue on the straight-line basis through the performance period.

A method based on output is preferred, since it most faithfully depicts the performance of the franchisor under the terms of a contract. However, an input-based method is certainly allowable if using it would be less costly for the franchisor, while still providing a reasonable proxy for the ongoing measurement of progress.

At the risk of oversimplifying the preceding rules, a franchisor should recognize revenue when it has substantially completed all tasks related to that revenue, as specified in the franchise agreement. Thus, initial franchise fees will probably be recognized by the franchisor shortly after a franchise location has been opened. Until that recognition has occurred, a franchise fee is recorded with the following journal entry:

	Debit	Credit
Cash [asset]	xxx	
Deferred revenue [liability]		xxx

The situation is more complex when an area development franchising agreement is involved. In this case, the franchisor is essentially receiving an advance payment on the fees that would otherwise have been paid upon the later opening of the individual units covered by the franchising agreement. Thus, the fee received should be classified as a deferred revenue liability, as was the case for the franchise fee associated with an individual unit. The liability can be converted into revenue as the franchisor substantially completes its obligations related to each unit linked to the agreement.

EXAMPLE

Bigelow Burgers enters into an area development franchising agreement with Anonymous Partners in exchange for an $80,000 fee. The agreement states that Anonymous must open a total of eight Bigelow locations over the ten-year term of the agreement. Bigelow initially records the $80,000 payment as follows:

	Debit	Credit
Cash [asset]	80,000	
Deferred revenue [liability]		80,000

After one year, Anonymous opens two Burger locations, allowing Bigelow to fulfill its obligation to find locations, secure leases, train employees, and assist with the store openings. This allows Bigelow to recognize the $10,000 of revenue associated with each store, using the following entry:

	Debit	Credit
Deferred revenue [liability]	20,000	
Franchise fees [revenue]		20,000

When the franchisor receives a transfer fee from an outgoing franchisee, the franchisor will likely be contractually obligated to provide initial support services to the replacement franchisee. Accordingly, the franchisor can only recognize the transfer fee as revenue after it has provided those services.

When the franchisor receives a franchise renewal fee from a franchisee, the related revenue recognition is the same as was used for the recognition of the initial franchise fee.

The Practical Expedient

A practical expedient is available for revenue recognition by a franchisor that is not a publicly-held business. In this situation, a franchisor that enters into a franchise agreement may account for the following pre-opening services as being distinct from the franchise license:

- Assistance in selection of a site
- Assistance in obtaining facilities and preparing the facilities for their intended use, including related financing, architectural, and engineering services, and lease negotiation
- Training of the franchisee's personnel or the franchisee
- Preparation and distribution of manuals and similar material concerning operations, administration, and record keeping
- Bookkeeping, information technology, and advisory services, including setting up the franchisee's records and advising the franchisee about income, real estate, and other taxes or about regulations affecting the franchisee's business
- Inspection, testing, and other quality control programs

When taking the practical expedient, a franchisor can make an accounting policy election to account for these pre-opening services as a single performance obligation, or decide whether they are distinct from one another and so should be accounted for separately. The usual outcome of this election is that a franchisor lumps all qualifying pre-opening services together into a single performance obligation.

This practical expedient applies only to the identification of performance obligations. It should be applied consistently to contracts with similar characteristics and in similar circumstances.

Franchisee Revenue Recognition

The revenue recognition criteria for a franchisor are well-defined, because they apply to a set of franchise fees that are broadly applicable across all types of franchising operations. This is not the case for the franchisee, which may be operating in any of a broad range of industries. Examples of the industries in which franchisees may operate include restaurants, trash removal, spas, fitness, plumbing, and home inspections. Depending on the industry, revenue recognition may occur at the point of sale or when a specific service is performed, or recognition may occur over a more protracted period. Despite the possible range of diversity in how a franchisee services its customers, the same five-step revenue recognition pattern described in the preceding section is still applicable. The franchisee needs to associate a contract with a specific customer, note the related performance obligations, determine pricing, match the pricing to the underlying performance obligations, and then recognize revenue as the various obligations are fulfilled. See the author's *Revenue Recognition* course for more information.

Presentation and Disclosures

In this section, we note franchise-specific cases that may require special presentation or disclosure in the financial statements.

Franchisor Presentation

A franchisor should clarify in its income statement the different types of revenue being generated by its franchise operations. A sample presentation is:

(000s)	20X3	20X2	20X1
Franchise royalties	$142,000	$138,000	$134,000
Franchise fees and other	8,000	4,000	2,000
Total franchise revenues	$150,000	$142,000	$136,000

When a franchisor has acquired a franchisee and is holding the related assets for sale, the recorded amount of the assets should be classified as a current asset on the balance sheet. A sample presentation is:

	20X3	20X2	20X1
Assets held for sale	$1,210,000	$970,000	$2,713,000

When a franchisor maintains a franchisee advertising fund and it is sufficiently large to be stated on the company's balance sheet, it is typically classified as a current liability, to reflect the fact that the funds are to be used within the next year. A sample balance sheet presentation is:

	20X3	20X2	20X1
Current liabilities:			
Franchise advertising liability	$400,000	$375,000	$360,000

Franchisee Presentation

When a franchisee records an initial franchise fee as an asset, it appears on the balance sheet as franchise rights, net of amortization. A sample presentation is:

	20X3	20X2	20X1
Franchise rights, net	$80,000	$90,000	$100,000

Franchisor Disclosures

A franchisor should state its accounting policy for recognizing revenue from its franchisees. For example:

> The Company collects royalties from each retail franchise based on a percentage of retail store gross sales. The Company recognizes royalties as revenue when earned. The Company collects initial franchise fees when franchise agreements are signed and recognizes the initial franchise fees as revenue when the franchise is opened, which is when the Company has performed substantially all initial services required by the franchise agreement.

When a franchisor experiences significant changes in the number of either franchised outlets or franchisor-owned outlets, it should disclose the following information:

- The number of franchises sold
- The number of franchises purchased in the period
- The number of franchised outlets currently in operation
- The number of franchisor-owned outlets currently in operation

For example:

> The following table summarizes the changes in the number of company-owned and franchise Lethal Sushi restaurants over the past three years:

	20X3	20X2	20X1
Company-operated restaurants:			
Beginning of period	367	322	310
New	23	35	17
Refranchised	--	--	--
Closed	-5	-4	-5
Acquired from franchisees	--	14	--
End of period total	385	367	322
Percent of system	53%	53%	49%
Franchise restaurants:			
Beginning of period	332	339	328
New	19	18	22
Refranchised	--	--	--
Closed	-10	-11	-11
Sold to company	--	-14	--
End of period total	341	332	339
Percent of system	47%	47%	51%
System end of period total	726	699	661

In addition, the franchisor should disclose the nature of all significant commitments associated with franchise agreements. This disclosure should describe the services to be provided that have not yet been substantially performed. For example:

> The Company is a guarantor under 30 franchisee property leases, with lease terms expiring on various dates through 20X0, and is the primary lessee on five franchisee property leases, which it subleases to them. The Company is fully liable for all obligations under the terms of the leases in the event that franchisees fail to pay the sums due under the leases.

If a franchisor regularly engages in the sale of company-owned or repossessed units, it should state its policy for how it accounts for these transactions. For example:

> The Company records gains or losses on the sale of its outlets in operating income when all stipulated conditions associated with the transactions have been met. Gains or losses are recorded in operating income, because the Company considers these transactions to be a recurring part of its operations.

A related issue is describing how the franchisor accounts for the assets related to any company-owned or repossessed units that it then sells to a franchisee. For example:

> When the Company owns an outlet, all related assets, liabilities, revenue, and expenses associated with that outlet are included in the Company's financial statements. When such a store is franchised, the net carrying values of the assets transferred to the franchisee are included in the cost of sales and services associated with the transfer.

When a franchisor operates a cooperative advertising fund with its franchisees, it should disclose the accounting for the fund. For example:

> The Company administers marketing funds which include contractual contributions. Contributions are recorded from franchisees as a liability until such funds are expended. The contributions to the marketing funds are designated for sales and marketing-related initiatives and advertising, and we act as an agent for the franchisees with regard to these contributions. Therefore, we do not reflect franchisee contributions to the funds in our consolidated statements of earnings.

> The following table summarizes contribution rates into the fund for both franchisee and Company-owned units:

20X3	20X2	20X1
3.9%	3.8%	3.7%

If a franchisor elects to use the practical expedient as described earlier in this manual, it should disclose that fact. In particular, if it makes the accounting policy election to recognize pre-opening services as a single performance obligation, it should disclose that fact.

Franchisee Disclosures

A franchisee should state its accounting policy for the recognition of fees paid for franchise agreements. For example:

> Fees for initial franchises and renewals are amortized using the straight-line method over the term of the agreement, which is generally twenty years.

Summary

There is comparatively little information in generally accepted accounting principles that is specifically targeted at the accounting for franchise operations. Nonetheless, this manual has shown that there are many unique aspects of franchise operations for which special accounting entries should be formalized, so that they can be employed on a recurring basis to generate consistent financial reporting.

Glossary

A

Amortize. The process of writing off the book value of an asset over its useful life.

Area franchise. A legal agreement that transfers the rights to a franchise for a specific geographic region, in which multiple franchise locations can be opened.

B

Business combination. A transaction in which an acquirer gains control of another business.

C

Carrying amount. The recorded cost of an asset, net of any accumulated depreciation or accumulated impairment losses.

Continuing franchise fees. The ongoing fees charged by a franchisor to a franchisee in exchange for the continuing rights granted under a franchise agreement.

Contra asset. A negative asset account that reduces the balance in the asset account with which it is paired.

Cooperative advertising fund. A fund that contains contributed funds from franchisees, to be used by the franchisor to purchase advertising on behalf of the franchisees.

F

Fair market value. The price that two parties are willing to pay for an asset, when both parties are well informed about the condition of the item, there is no undue pressure to buy or sell, and there is no time pressure to complete the deal.

Franchise. A privilege granted to market a good or service, usually under a trademarked name.

Franchise agreement. A contract that defines the relationship between a franchisor and franchisee, defines the rights transferred, the contributions of both parties to the maintenance of a franchise, the marketing practices to be followed, and the related fee structure.

Franchisee. A party that runs a purchased franchise for a specific location.

Franchisor. A party that grants business rights related to a franchise to a franchisee.

G

Goodwill. The excess of the purchase price paid for an acquired entity and the amount of the price not assigned to acquired assets and liabilities.

I

Impairment. A permanent decline in the value of an asset.

Initial franchise fee. The fee paid to a franchisor in exchange for establishing a franchise relationship, along with the provision of some initial services.

Initial services. The provision of services and advice to a franchisee, as stated in the initial franchise agreement.

M

Master franchising agreement. An agreement in which the franchisor grants another party the right to sub-franchise to an additional level of franchisees.

Index

www.ingramcontent.com/pod-product-compliance
Lightning Source LLC
Chambersburg PA
CBHW051431200326
41520CB00023B/7429